Sitting on Death Row

The Most Notorious Cases of Death Row Killers Vol.2

Jack Smith

All rights reserved. © 2020 by Jack Smith and Maplewood Publishing. No part of this publication or the information in it may be quoted from or reproduced in any form by means such as printing, scanning, photocopying, or otherwise without prior written permission of the copyright holder.

Efforts have been made to ensure that the information in this book is accurate and complete. However, the author and the publisher do not warrant the accuracy of the information, text, and graphics contained within the book due to the rapidly changing nature of science, research, known and unknown facts, and the internet. The author and the publisher do not hold any responsibility for errors, omissions, or contrary interpretation of the subject matter herein. This book is presented solely for motivational and informational purposes only.

Warning
Throughout the book, there are some descriptions of murders and crime scenes that some people might find disturbing. There might be also some language used by people involved in the murders that may not be appropriate.

Note
Words in italic are quoted words from verbatim and have been reproduced as is, including any grammatical errors and misspelled words.

ISBN: 9798583617517

Printed in the United States

Contents

Mitigating Circumstances	1
Frank Abbandando	3
Tom Odle	11
Betty Lou Beets	19
Robert Alton Harris	33
George James Trepal	37
Karla Faye Tucker	45
Joseph Carl Shaw	51
Timothy Joseph McGhee	55
Emilia Carr	61
Darlie Routier	69
Spencer Goodman	75
The Last Resort	81
Further Readings	83

Mitigating Circumstances

Perhaps this is risking an understatement, but the fact that some states reserve the right to end our lives is a very serious thing. In those places, this ultimate punishment is reserved for those who have not only committed a terrible crime, but whose mitigating circumstances around that crime are so horrendous that it has been deemed that their life should be brought to an end. It's a tall order to make, but some crimes are just so bad that their mitigating circumstances seem to merit it. Just take, for example, the case of Timothy McGhee.

Mr. McGhee was a gang banger in California in the late 1990s and early 2000s who terrorized the greater Los Angeles area. He killed at will and had others kill on his orders. He shot rival gangsters as well as random people on the street, leaving at least 12 people dead in his wake. He also orchestrated an elaborate ambush to kill police officers who simply dared to pursue criminals who had sought refuge on his supposed turf. And once behind bars, the first thing McGhee did was cause a prison riot that left numerous people injured and nearly killed a member of the prison staff. For someone like McGhee, reform and rehabilitation do not seem to be an option.

On the other hand, a case like that of Betty Lou Beets is not notorious so much for the number of people killed or injured, as much as the sheer callous nature in which this killer manipulated and killed not strangers or enemies—but those who loved and cared for her. Before her execution on death row, Ms. Beets had been married several times and was quite skilled at luring men not only to her bed but also to their death.

As you can see, the circumstances of every murder are different, and it's the mitigating circumstances therein that might lead to a life or death sentence for those involved. Here in this book, we'll take a look at the latter. Herein, you will find some of the most notorious cases to ever end up on death row.

Frank Abbandando

Who: Frank Abbandando
Nickname: The Dasher
When: 1930s
Where: New York
Number of suspected victims: At least 40
Apprehension: 1940

Background

Frank Abbandando was the son of Italian immigrants who came to New York in the early 20th century. Born on July 11, 1910, he was part of a big family with 11 other siblings. From the very beginning, Frank had to fight for every crumb he was given in life. Growing up poor on the wrong side of the tracks certainly wasn't easy, and it wasn't long before Frank turned to crime.

By the time of his adolescence, he was committing extortion against local businesses, demanding money lest he would burn down their property. Shortly thereafter, he hooked up with a street gang in Brooklyn. He rose through the ranks of this outfit fairly quickly, becoming a lieutenant of a local gang leader known as Harry "Happy" Maione. (He was called "Happy" sarcastically, due to his grim and serious demeanor.)

It was under Maione's tutelage that Abbandando further perfected his skills in racketeering, organized gambling, loan sharking, and extortion. The young man continued to work for the gang until he was arrested in 1928 for attacking one of New York's finest.

For his assault on a member of the NYPD, Abbandando was sent off to a reform school. Located in Elmira, New York, the school specialized in taking ruffians like Abbandando and teaching them a thing or two about life. It's not clear how much reforming Abbandando actually achieved, but he was fondly remembered as a good baseball player on the school team. In fact, on the baseball field, he would earn a nickname that would stick with him for the rest of his life; they called him the "Dasher" because of his speed.

However, the name would come to take on a whole other meaning when he returned to the criminal world. Shortly after Frank returned from reform school, he was recruited by an NYC crime syndicate which would later become known by the media as "Murder, Inc." Through Murder, Inc., Abbandando would become a hired hitman.

Still working for Harry Maione, he continued to be involved in racketeering, gambling, and loan sharking. In 1931, Abbandando and Maione hooked up with Abe "Kid Twist" Reles so they could squeeze another group of thugs led by the Shapiro Brothers out of the tough section of NYC known as Brownsville, and then take over their business.

Reles used to work with the Shapiro Brothers but had a falling out with them, at which point he went on the offensive. Reles befriended an operative of the Shapiro Brothers—a guy named Joey Silvers. He persuaded Silvers to give him inside information about the Shapiro Brothers' movements.

Little did Reles know, however, that after he agreed to help them, Silvers double-crossed Reles and went right to his bosses to tell them what Reles was up to. Instead of getting the drop on the Shapiro Brothers, Silvers arranged for the Shapiro Brothers to ambush Reles. Abe Reles barely escaped getting killed. The Shapiros were not through with him, however; Meyer Shapiro would seek vengeance in the most despicable of ways.

In a spate of personally targeted revenge, Meyer abducted Reles' girlfriend. He grabbed her off the street, shoved her into his car, and drove off to a remote location. He then proceeded to beat and sexually assault her. When he was through, Meyers shoved her out into the street and told her to tell Abe Reles all about what he had done.

Even though Reles himself was a hardened criminal, when he found out what had happened to his girlfriend he was horrified. It's said that he became insane with rage, and he plotted his revenge against the Shapiro Brothers. In this, he consulted with Frank Abbandando's old partner, Harry Maione. Maione agreed to help Reles, and together they formed a task force that would include Frank Abbandando as one of their hitmen.

The Shapiro Brothers – Meyer, Irving, and William – basically ran this part of NYC. They had a monopoly over all the prostitution, extortion, and protection rackets in Brownsville. They also controlled the gambling – especially the popular slot machine business – raking in a ton of illicit dough. Taking them out, therefore, would not only satisfy Reles' need for revenge – but it would also put Reles and his cronies in charge of Brownsville.

The Crimes

The first Shapiro brother to be taken out by Murder, Inc., was Irving. Reles confronted him at his apartment building and shot him numerous times. The next Shapiro brother to be cornered was the one who had wronged Abe Reles the most – Meyer Shapiro. Meyer was cornered by Reles, Abbandando, and another man at a speakeasy. Any one of the three could have killed him, but it's believed that they allowed Reles to do the honors.

Shortly after this hit, Reles then tracked down the treacherous Joey Silvers and killed him as well. It would take another few years before the group was able to get to the last living Shapiro brother, Willie. In 1934, Willie was finally located by the group and sent to the grave just like his brothers. In this case, they beat him badly and buried him – an autopsy later revealed that he was still alive at the time.

After the Shapiro brothers were wiped out, Reles and company became the dominant force in Brownsville, New York. At this point, a guy named Louis Capone, who owned popular restaurants and had deep connections with the Mafia, put Reles in contact with high-ranking members of the mob. From this point forward, Murder, Inc. would be the "enforcement arm" of the main vein of organized crime in New York.
Frank Abbandando married a hairdresser named Jennie DeLuca, and they had two sons, Lawrence, in 1927, and

Frank Jr. in 1935. (Both appear to have been involved in organized crime their whole lives, and both were killed in the 1990s.)

Over the next few years, Frank Abbandando would become the most ruthless hitman of the group. It's believed that he killed at least 40 people over the next few years. As far as hired murderers go, Abbandando was known to be a professional. He was efficient, he got the job done, and he didn't ask any questions. If a mob boss ordered him to make a hit, he just did it. He often used an ice pick.

For each contract killing, Abbandando was allegedly given about $500. This was a pretty good chunk of change back in the 1930s. With this cash, he bought fancy clothes, fancy cars, and he wined and dined with beautiful women. This sociopath apparently had no conscience whatsoever about those whose lives he had taken, as long as their deaths continued to foot the bill for his extravagant lifestyle.

It all came to an end, however, in 1940, when Murder, Inc.'s ringleader, Reles, was arrested on charges related to a cold case murder. Reles was apparently caught off guard by his arrest, and in a bid to save his own skin, he readily flipped on the other members of Murder, Inc., implicating Abbandando in a wide variety of crimes. In the end, the charge that stuck was the killing of one George Rudnick in Brownsville, which had occurred on May 25, 1937.

Once the trial convened, Frank was shocked to find his former boss testifying against him. Reles explained in graphic detail how Abbandando had killed Rudnick. Rudnick was apparently a loan shark in Brownsville, and back in 1937 had come under the suspicion of Murder, Inc. of being an informant to the police. According to Reles, this was why Abbandando and his cohorts stabbed Rudnick some 63 times with an ice pick before choking him to death and then finishing it all off by crushing his head with a meat cleaver.

When it was Abbandando's turn to take the stand, he denied having anything at all to do with the killing. In the meantime, he took every opportunity to curse Reles and even managed to whisper a threat to the judge, Franklin W. Taylor, prompting the police to stand guard between Taylor and Abbandando. Nevertheless, Judge Taylor proved that he had nerves of steel and was not going to be pushed around by this street bully. The trial proceeded.

The prosecution presented several killings Abbandando was accused of taking part in, including a high-profile hit on a guy named Feliz Esposito on February 9, 1939. Prosecutors also brought up an insidious incident in which Abbandando and his goons reportedly abducted a 17-year-old woman from a nightclub in Brownsville and raped her.

Abbandando was quick to deny all charges. Especially when he was linked to organized crime figures, he claimed complete ignorance. This was most likely because he thought he still had a get-out-of-jail-free card through his connections in the mob. He wasn't going to flip like Reles; instead, he was willing to play the part of the loyal soldier, hoping to be rewarded by having a few strings pulled to reduce or beat the charges against him.

During the trial, it was apparent to all that Abbandando did not take the proceedings seriously and he didn't seem too concerned about his fate. His demeanor showed his belief that he could beat the system. He often smiled at the press and it seemed as if he really thought he was going to get away with murder.

Investigation and Sentence

Frank Abbandando was ultimately found guilty of murder and sentenced to death. It's said that even on the way to the electric chair on February 19, 1942, Abbandando still seemed convinced that someone would somehow spring him out and there would be a last-minute reprieve. This was not the case, and Frank Abbandando was executed without any delay.

Update

After the death of Frank Abbandando, Murder, Inc. was disbanded. The mafia learned that outsourcing contract killings with mobsters outside the main branch was too risky. From then on, they strictly used only mafia members for conducting hits.

Tom Odle

Who: Tom Odle
When: November 8, 1985
Where: Illinois
Number of victims: 5
Apprehension: November 9, 1985

Background

Tom Odle makes our list of death row killers for the crime of murdering his whole family. At one time, he was the youngest criminal to ever be sentenced to death, but in 2003, his sentence was commuted to life in prison.

He was born into a dysfunctional and abusive family. But according to Tom, his mother Carolyn made his life a living hell while his father Robert just stood idly by and allowed the abuse to happen.

Tom claims that when he was a child, his mother was extremely strict and most of the time he was forced to stay in his room. He also contends that he wasn't allowed to play with other children. He could not go to their houses and he was not allowed to have them over to his. Tom was the oldest child in his family, followed by a sister named Robyn, a brother named Sean, and then another brother named Scott.

According to Tom, the only child his mom was particularly nice to was his sister, Robyn. Since he was the oldest, Tom had to pick up his mother's slack as a parent, and was forced to babysit and take care of his younger siblings – a fact that he greatly resented. He says his mother beat him for the smallest of infractions – sometimes for just playing too loudly. She demanded that her children be completely quiet, and the slightest of sounds would provoke her wrath.

While all of this was going on, Carolyn was presenting a façade of not just normalcy, but of being a perfect parent. She was even the president of the PTO.

However, even though Tom claims his mother was a harsh disciplinarian at home, she was quite different in public. Once Tom became disruptive at school and started to get into fights with his classmates, Carolyn was his staunchest supporter. She would defend her son's actions, claiming that he was being bullied and had every right to defend himself.

This firm support is in stark contrast with what Tom claims went on behind closed doors, so either Tom is telling the truth and his mother lived a double life, presenting herself as a respectable, loving parent in public, while being an abuser at home – or Tom is lying to justify his own actions.

One must remember that since Carolyn and the rest of Tom's immediate family are dead, Tom is the only one who can testify. No one else will ever tell their side of the story. So could someone charged with killing his whole family be fabricating his past to make himself look like a victim? It's possible, but there were apparently some outward signs of abuse during his childhood that can indeed be corroborated. At one point, Tom's younger brother, Sean, was removed from the home because he talked about his mother withholding food and chaining him to the bed when she went out. The parents were forced to take a parenting class.

Additionally, some friends and family did occasionally question Carolyn as to why she was so strict with Tom. Her apparent answer to all this was that she was trying to keep him out of trouble – that she was trying to avoid raising a juvenile delinquent. Well, if that were the case, her mission was an absolute failure, because by the time Tom was in high school and had finally gained a social life of his own, he was hanging out with a pretty rough and rowdy crowd.

He was getting drunk and high on a regular basis, and with his newfound crew, he began to break into houses to steal and pawn valuables and get cash to feed his drug habit. He admits this much. So whatever may have occurred in his childhood, by the time he was a teenager, he was on a decidedly wrong path in life, one of his own making.

His crimes first caught up with him his sophomore year of high school when he was arrested for possessing stolen goods. Since he was a minor he got off relatively easy, with just a slap on the wrist. It was hoped that getting busted would serve as a warning to Tom and get him to clean up his act. But it wouldn't be long before his misbehavior would become downright deadly.

The Crimes

Just before he murdered his whole family, Tom was on the verge of being kicked out of his parents' home. They had tried to get him to quit doing drugs and get a job, but since he didn't seem to be willing to do so, they decided he couldn't stay. You can call it tough love—but they apparently thought it was the only way to get their little birdie to fly right.

Tom's deadline for moving out was set for November 8. His parents had come to the conclusion that kicking him out of the house and forcing him to get a job and support himself was the best thing to do.

Tom's testimony was that he woke up that morning to find his dad at the table having breakfast, and he had the sudden compulsion to grab a knife. He claims he wasn't thinking of killing anyone in that moment, it was just a strange, unexplainable urge to grab a knife that was hanging on a rack on the kitchen wall. And so, while his father's eyes were elsewhere, he swiped the knife and left the room.

He still wasn't sure what he was going to do with it, and at one point he even went back into the kitchen to put it back on the rack, but his father was moving around in the room, so he had to back away, lest he would be seen with the blade. According to Tom, he then headed to the living room to stash the knife behind the couch, but he says he kept hearing a voice in his head that insisted he use the knife on his father.

At this point, he turned around and headed back to the kitchen. He says he blacked out shortly thereafter, and the next thing he consciously recalls was standing in front of his father, who was bleeding heavily from a knife wound to the neck. His dying father said something about needing to get help before he slipped out of his chair and fell dead onto the floor.

Tom then scrambled to clean up all of the blood on the floor and dragged his father's body into a bathroom. It was shortly after he finished this grisly task his mother came home. Tom prepared to ambush her by hiding behind the door where he knew she would enter. And sure enough, as soon as she came in the door, he leaped out at her with the knife. He slashed at her throat, and his terrified mother ran into the living room with Tom chasing her and slashing at her neck as she ran.

She managed to finally put some distance between the two of them and, according to Tom, she threw her car keys at him and asked if he was trying to kill her. Carolyn then collapsed and died shortly thereafter.

The next victim was Tom's brother, Scott. Tom waited for the boy to come home from school. At first, they just sat and talked, but when Scott started asking questions about where their parents were, Tom had to make up excuses as to why they weren't there. Tom then turned on his brother and began to choke him. He tried to literally squeeze the life out of the little boy with his bare hands. When this didn't work, he grabbed a nearby piece of clothing and wrapped it around the child's throat to strangle him to death.

That left his sister Robyn and brother Sean. He got in his dad's car and drove to their school to pick them up. It was upon entering their home that the horror show would begin. Tom attacked Sean first, brutally stabbing him several times before turning the blade on his sister.

After single-handedly murdering his whole family in this fashion, Tom then went on a joyride with some of his friends, driving around in his father's car, drinking and smoking weed. Eventually, he ended up at a local roach motel with his friend Larry, Larry's girlfriend Kim, and his own girlfriend, Theresa.

The group continued to do drugs and drink at the hotel. Later that night, Tom gave Larry and Kim a ride home, and upon his return at the motel, Tom and Theresa just hung out and watched movies together on the motel's crusty old television.

According to Tom, at this point, he started to think that the slaying of his parents hadn't actually happened. He felt like it was all just a "bad trip," a nightmare sequence that looped on repeat in his mind. It just didn't seem real.

He would be in for a rude awakening the next morning, however, when Theresa phoned a friend from the hotel room, who subsequently informed her that the cops were on the lookout for them.

Investigation and Sentence

Tom and his girlfriend Theresa tried to leave the motel that morning but were immediately intercepted by police who had tracked them down and were waiting for them. As soon as Tom and Theresa stepped out and walked toward his father's car, police rushed forward with guns drawn and placed them under arrest. Upon his arrival at the jail, Tom was placed in an interrogation room where detectives proceeded to grill him about what had happened.

It only took a few minutes of questioning before Tom began to confess to the crime in its entirety.

As Tom sat in jail awaiting his trial on November 26, 1985, the county coroner ruled the obvious – that all the family members were the victims of homicide. The coroner who examined the victims would later play a pivotal role during the course of Tom's trial, providing vivid testimony as to just how brutally the family was killed, and giving graphic descriptions of the many stab wounds and other injuries family members had sustained.
On May 29, 1986, a jury found Tom guilty of murdering his family, and he was given a death sentence. However, this

death sentence was halted in the year 2000, when Illinois governor, George Ryan, imposed a moratorium on the death penalty. Just a few years later, Tom's death sentence was commuted to life imprisonment without parole.

Update

After his death sentence was overturned, Tom Odle began to reflect more deeply upon his actions and reached out to psychologist and author Robert Hanlon to explore why he did what he did. It was these consultations that resulted in the 2013 book, *Survived by One: The Life and Mind of a Family Mass Murderer.*

The prevailing theme has been Tom shifting much of the blame for his deeds onto his parents' alleged mistreatment of him, as well as his drug-addled mind. This book seems to be Odle's attempt to seriously consider his actions. Yet in the end, he still seems unable of accepting full responsibility for what he did, and he still has times when he feels like he's going to wake up from a bad dream.

Betty Lou Beets

Who: Betty Lou Beets
Nickname:
When: Late 1970s and Early 1980s
Where: Texas
Number of victims: 2 murders, 1 attempted murder
Apprehension:

Background

Betty Lou Beets would become infamous in Texas, but she began her life in North Carolina. She was born on March 12, 1937, to a poor family who struggled to make a living as sharecroppers. Her parents, James and Louise Dunevant, owned a modest cabin. The home had no running water, no electricity, and didn't even have the luxury of glass windows.

It was a primitive and desolate existence, for sure. Food was often scarce and the family was forced to survive on rations of flour, salt pork, and cornmeal. Her parents' sharecropping work had them cultivating tobacco fields all season long – and then, once wintertime had arrived, her mother would take on a job as a house servant, making low wages cleaning the homes of the rich.

As Betty grew a little older, the family decided to move to the city of Danville, Virginia, leaving their sharecropping life behind in favor of work in the city's cotton factories. Here, they lived in a modest rental home, but they at least had electricity, heat, and running water. Just as things were beginning to look up, however, Betty began to suffer health problems. When she was three, she came down with the measles, and on several nights had a fever so high that her parents were afraid that they might lose her.

After recovering from the measles, she then began to be plagued by terrible ear infections that would eventually result in her being hearing impaired. Her difficulty hearing would cause her to struggle in the classroom, where she earned poor grades and was held back in the fourth grade. Betty was humiliated by this occurrence, and some say it would leave her bitter for the rest of her life.

When Betty was twelve, her mother suddenly had what was described as "a psychotic break with reality." She supposedly heard voices and began having hallucinations. When her mother was institutionalized, she had to leave school to look after her younger brother and sister. She essentially became a surrogate housewife for her father, having to cook and clean around the house.

Betty's home life soon became intolerable and she was searching for a way out – and at just 15 years of age, she believed she had found it. This was when she crossed paths with an 18-year-old boy by the name of Robert Franklin Branson. Robert, with his jet-black hair and winning grin, was both handsome and charming. Despite the fact that his job prospects were pretty meager – he had a job in a zipper factory – Betty saw a potential form of escape whenever she looked into his eyes.

For Betty and Robert, things moved pretty quickly and by July 18, 1952, they were married. Just one year later, Faye – Betty's first child – would be born. You might think that this would be a happy time for a young couple, but Betty began to change her mind about married life.

She disliked the responsibilities of motherhood and she complained about the lack of material comforts. She felt she was no better off than she had been caring for her younger siblings and cooking and cleaning for her father. Robert genuinely tried to make a better life for his family, and in search of a higher income, he went to work at Norfolk, Virginia's shipyard.

He thought the extra money would ease some of the burdens for his wife, but he was wrong. Betty simply felt too young to be trapped at home with an infant. While her former high school classmates were out having fun, she felt cheated. She wanted out. At this point, heated arguments began to erupt between her and her husband, which resulted in a six-month separation.

Betty then moved back in with her parents, but of course, this only aggravated her even more. As much as she felt like she was missing out as a stay-at-home wife with a baby, she felt a lot worse being separated with a baby, staying at the home of her parents. She ended up getting so depressed that she tried to take her own life by swallowing a couple of bottles of aspirin.

She recovered from the episode, but Betty's alarmed parents urged her estranged husband to come over and speak with her. They managed to smooth out their disagreements, and Betty agreed to go back with him to patch up their marriage. Betty had another child with Robert the following year, and since his family was beginning to grow, Robert decided that he needed even more money. His solution was to move the family over to Texas where he would work in construction.

They ended up moving to a small Texan town called Mesquite, just south of Dallas. The family would not just do well in Texas; they would thrive. In 14 years of marriage, the union would produce six happy and well-adjusted children. Amazingly, since she was so young when she herself got married to start this family, Betty was only 29 years of age after giving birth to this brood. She was also still quite attractive. She was slim with a nice figure, and with the help of her husband's hard work, she was able to wear nice clothes.

Also by this time, although she seemed by now to have accepted her fate, she had become bored enough to begin cheating on her husband. She would actually recruit her older daughters to watch the younger children while she would go to bars looking for men. When men admired her and told her how good she looked and how fun she was to be around, she finally received some of the attention she so desperately craved.

Eventually, however, her husband caught on and gave her an ultimatum. She had to quit her affairs and stay home, or else. Betty didn't stop. So, in 1969, her husband served her with divorce papers. The terms of the agreement allowed Betty to have custody of the children, and Robert agreed to pay $350 a month. It was a pretty generous deal, considering that it was Betty's cheating that brought the whole thing about. Nevertheless, Betty liked to play the victim and get sympathy and would frequently cry to her kids, "I still love and miss your daddy."

The kids, meanwhile, experienced a major change when their father left. Their mother, who had been at least a decent housewife, now seemed to let everything go. She was also gone much of the time, living it up at night because she was too depressed to stay home. Her kids didn't like the strain that they were under, and one by one sought means for escape.

First, her oldest daughter Faye followed in her mother's footsteps and got married at just 15 years of age just so she could get out of the house. Then her daughter Phyllis and son Robby opted to live with their father and the woman he had recently married. Her daughter Connie then decided to live with her sister Faye and her new husband. Her daughter Shirley began to bounce around from place to place, staying at friends' houses as much as possible, just so she wouldn't have to be home. Only her youngest child, Bobby, would tough it out and stay with his mother during this rocky period.

It was a year after her divorce from her first husband that Betty began to see a guy named Billy Lane. They got married on July 28, 1970. It turned out to be a rocky union at best and completely volatile at worst. Betty drank heavily, and now in her early 30s, began to abuse a weight-loss drug (Dexatrim) because she feared gaining weight. The combination made her irritable and quick to anger – and her husband retaliated by beating her.

As one might guess, the relationship did not last, and the two would part company before the year was even out. Even after the divorce, however, they engaged in an off-again, on-again relationship – that is, until January of 1972, when her Billy Lane turned up dead.

It all apparently started on January 17th, when Lane confronted Betty at a nightclub, apparently angry because she was dancing with another man. Betty stormed out of the club, and on the way home, she flagged down a police officer and told him that Billy was following her. The police officer agreed to escort her home. Then, around two in the morning, the police received a phone call from Betty. They responded, came to her home, and found Billy Lane lying unconscious in a pool of his own blood.

Police questioned Betty as to what happened and she claimed that she had shot her ex in self-defense. She told the police that he had come to her door in a belligerent rage and she had no choice but to pull the trigger. Betty's daughter Connie happened to be home that night and had witnessed at least part of the event. She partially corroborated her mother's story.

However, the police were skeptical of Betty's claims because Billy was shot from the back. This meant that he was not rushing to attack her as she claimed, but most likely trying to get away from her when she shot him. As a result, the police charged her with "assault with intention to commit murder with malice."

Billy, fortunately, survived his injuries, but unfortunately for Betty, his version of events was entirely different from hers.

According to him, he was at his adult daughter's house when Betty called and asked if he wanted to come over. She told him that she wanted to talk. He initially told her it was too late, and asked if it could wait until morning.

Betty insisted that she needed him to come over that night. Bill claimed that he was hesitant, but he obliged her and headed over to her apartment. But upon his arrival, something strange happened. As soon as he knocked on her door, Betty started screaming at him to leave and demanded that he leave her alone. It was as if it was an act she had rehearsed.

She wanted to trick him into showing up and then pretend (with her daughter Connie listening) that Bill was stalking her. Bill didn't know what to make of it, but when she flipped out on him, he immediately turned around and started to leave as directed. Bill claims that as soon as he turned his back to leave, Betty began shooting.

But the case against Betty ended up going nowhere because after Bill checked out of the hospital, he began a relationship with Betty again. It's hard to comprehend how a man would go back to the woman who shot him, but it's said that he truly was in love with Betty, and she had a way of charming him right out of his senses. To the disbelief of those involved in the case, he agreed to sign an affidavit claiming that he had threatened her.

With these mitigating circumstances adding to her case, Betty was able to enter into a plea deal and was slapped on the wrist with nothing more than a $100 fine – which her victim, Bill Lane, ended up paying for her. Incredibly, this "happy couple" then decided to remarry. This time around, it lasted less than a month.

Many who knew Betty felt that she had buttered Bill up and sweet-talked him into marrying her so he would agree to help her beat any serious charges for shooting him. At any rate, as soon as they split the second time.

Betty took off and moved to Little Rock, Arkansas. She was only there a short time before she met a man named Ronnie C. Threlkold and convinced him to move back to Texas with her.

The two set up house in Dallas and got married in the spring of 1978. As was the case in the past, it wasn't long before the relationship became extremely volatile. Towards the end, Betty even tried to run him over with her car. Needless to say, the marriage failed. By 1979 she was on the rebound again, looking for another man.

That man turned out to be a guy she met at a gas station: Doyle Wayne Barker. Barker had struck up a conversation with Betty and the next thing anyone knew, the two were married. It was fall, 1979. Sticking with her pattern of short-lived romances, the couple would then divorce in January of 1980...and decide to remarry shortly thereafter.

Barker seemed to have been infatuated with Betty, and like many men, he tried to butter her up and get in her good graces by buying things for her. He bought Betty a brand-new mobile home by a lake, which she really loved. The only trouble was that the property was in his name – so when Betty eventually wanted out of the marriage again, she had the quandary of not being able to divorce Barker without the risk of losing the trailer. This was the moment that murder truly came to mind.

The Crimes

According to Betty's daughter Shirley, when she wanted to end her relationship with Barker, Betty began openly joking about killing him. She even pointed out a hole dug in the yard where she planned to bury the man. Betty had apparently sweet-talked a construction worker to dig it, claiming she was going to use it for a barbecue pit when in reality she wanted a grave for her husband.

At the time, Shirley thought her mother was kidding, but she wasn't. Soon after this macabre joke, Betty crept into bed with her husband in the middle of the night. Using a pillow to silence the gun, she shot him multiple times and then dragged the man outside and buried him.

When people who knew Barker later asked about him, Betty claimed that he had run out on her and she didn't know where he was. This seemed highly illogical since Barker's truck was still parked in her driveway, but Betty stuck to the story.

Less than a year after Doyle disappeared, Betty met her next husband – Jimmy Don Beets. She met Jimmy at the bar where she was waitressing at the time, and they married in August of 1982. Just like all of her other marriages, it didn't take long for her volatility to emerge.

On the evening of August 5, 1983, Jimmy's boat was discovered by employees and patrons of the Redwood Marina, aimlessly drifting in the water. Fellow boaters Tex Beaucamp and Gabby Harrison rowed out to investigate and saw what they thought was an abandoned boat. But upon closer inspection, they found personal items that most people would not simply leave behind, such as a fishing license.

This license identified the owner of the boat to be Jimmy Don Beets. He was well known in the local community since he was the captain of the Dallas Fire Department at the time.

There was no sign of Jimmy anywhere. After figuring out who the boat belonged to, Gabby and Tex hauled it back to the dock, where a crowd was already waiting for them. The curious onlookers were all likewise saddened to learn that the fire captain's boat had been found abandoned with its occupant missing. Observant witnesses also happened to notice that something was not quite right about the boat: a propeller was missing.

At first, it was considered an accident. It was theorized that perhaps the boat had hit something that knocked off the blade. As the investigation into Jimmy's disappearance continued, however, this would prove to be a crucial piece of information. At this point, the owner of the marina, Lil Smith, took over and grabbed a phone book to find the number of the missing fisherman. Dialing up an entry listed as J. D. Beets, she waited patiently as the phone call went through.

After several rings, however, she had to hang up. It took her a few more tries, but finally, a woman picked up the phone.

It was then that the owner informed Betty Lou Beets that her husband's empty boat was found floating empty in the water. Betty Lou shouted into the phone that Jimmy had gone fishing the day before and that she had been so worried.

Betty Lou had apparently already informed the police that her husband was missing, and just a few minutes after hanging up with Lil Smith, Betty was right there in the office of the marina. Upon her arrival on the scene, she asked to see the boat. She was obliged, and as soon as she laid eyes on it, she gasped in surprise, as she asked, "What on earth could have happened to him?"

She then referred to the damaged motor, and talked about how he was always fixing things for other people, but lately, his own motor had been giving him trouble. And though nobody had asked about his health, she mentioned that he'd had a heart attack, five years before.

At first glance, her words seemed to corroborate evidence found at the scene, since there were several pill bottles of nitroglycerin, an agent commonly prescribed for heart attack patients, rolling around on the bottom of the boat. Could Mr. Beets have simply had a heart attack and fallen into the water? That's what Mrs. Beets seemed to think – or at least that's what she seemed to want everyone else to think.

Was this all a rehearsed stunt? Lil Smith was quite amazed at how calm Betty was. Yes, she did express surprise, but the surprise seemed to wear off rather quickly, and what struck Lil as particularly strange was the fact that there were no tears in Betty's eyes.

Investigation and Sentence

After Betty called the police to report that her husband was missing, and then the marina discovered the abandoned boat, the investigation into what may have befallen Mr. Beets began. These efforts would be led by Sheriff Charlie Fields, who arrived shortly thereafter. He surveyed the abandoned boat and the items left behind by the missing man. Soon, he noticed literal storm clouds on the horizon and called off the search. He told those around him, "There'll be no search tonight, boys, not with this storm brewing."

As soon as the sun came up the next day, however, investigators, along with family, friends, and 50 firefighters who had worked with Jimmy in the past, were back at the docks looking for the missing man. The coast guard also arrived at the lake to scan the waters for any sign of him. Betty, meanwhile, was at the lake without fail to oversee the entire operation.

She often thanked the investigators for their efforts, but she seemed insincere to many. As the search became more and more difficult, rumors of foul play began to be whispered. Captain Blackburn later said that he doubted that Jimmy had drowned and that something just wasn't right about the situation.

And after the investigation used the resources of some 200 boats, two helicopters, four airplanes, and hundreds of volunteers, many others began to agree. After 13 days, the official search was called off. It was clear that wherever Beets was, he was not in the lake. So, what happened to him? Despite the massive search, Betty Lou Beets seemed ready to plan the funeral before his body was even found. Just a couple of days into the search, she had actually gone to a funeral home and picked out a white casket lined with blue satin, as well as a cemetery plot for her missing husband.

Betty Lou Beets was ultimately arrested on June 8th, 1985, about two years after her husband had gone missing. A search warrant was issued that allowed access to Betty Lou's property. Here, the bodies of both Jimmy Beets and Doyle Barker were discovered. Investigators then found the murder weapon: a pistol whose bullets undeniably matched those found in the bodies of both men.

Betty's children began to flip on her and divulge information about how they had witnessed events or helped Betty dispose of the bodies. Her son Bobby even revealed that he was the one who planted Jimmy Beets' belongings in the boat before sending the vessel afloat at the marina so that it would be assumed that Jimmy had drowned.

Incredibly, this sociopathic mother then decided to flip on her own children, and concocted a story in which she alleged that it was her kids who were the real killers, who had pressured her into aiding them and covering up the crime.

Her children had no reason to kill her two former husbands, and the jurors – as almost anyone would – considered her allegations absolutely absurd. Although she was not tried for the killing of Doyle Wayne Barker, the jury rendered a guilty verdict for the killing of Jimmy Don Beets. And for this crime, she was sentenced to death.

Update

Betty appealed the decision of the courts for well over a decade, but all this pleading came to an end on February 24, 2000, when 62-year-old Betty – who had grandchildren and even great-grandchildren – was executed.

Robert Alton Harris

Who: Robert Alton Harris
When: 1978
Where: California
Number of victims: 2
Apprehension: 1979

Background

He began life in the conservative auspices of Fort Bragg, North Carolina, the fifth of nine children. His father, Kenneth, was a war veteran, an alcoholic, and an abuser. His mother, Evelyn, was a housewife. When Evelyn was pregnant with Robert, in fact, his father had kicked his mom in the stomach during a drunken rage. This assault actually induced labor and caused baby Robert to be born prematurely.

Some would later cite this incident as a possible contributing factor to Robert's unusual behavior as if it somehow contributed to his troubled mental state. At any rate, Robert found himself on the wrong side of the law at a young age – when he was just 13 years old, he was apprehended for stealing a car and sent to juvenile detention.

Robert was obviously troubled and his own family did not provide him with much support to aid in his reform. His mother ended up abandoning him. Nevertheless, by the time he was a young adult, he managed to temporarily straighten his life out. He grew up, got married, had a kid, and worked a normal job.

However, in 1975, his life would once again spiral out of control. In California, Harris got into a fight with one of his brother's friends – and actually beat that man to death. For this, he was charged and found guilty of voluntary manslaughter. He would only end up serving a few years of his sentence, however, getting out on parole in 1978.

Shortly after he was sprung from jail in 1978, his real rampage would begin.

The Crimes

Fresh out of prison in June of 1978, Robert hooked up with his younger brother Daniel and began plotting to rob a bank. Daniel aided his brother by breaking into a neighbor's home and stealing a couple of guns for the task. Before the robbery took place, however, they committed a truly senseless crime. On July 5th, they came across two teenaged boys – Michael Baker and John Mayeski – just hanging out, munching on a couple of burgers in the parking lot of a local fast-food joint. Robert got the idea to steal their vehicle.

Robert approached the vehicle. Brandishing his weapon, he ordered them to let him into the cab before telling the driver to take him out to Miramar Lake. The startled young men did as directed, and Robert's brother followed closely behind in his own car. Robert assured his prey that they would not be harmed. Yet as soon as they were parked, he marched both young men out of the vehicle at gunpoint and ordered them to kneel.

Despite his promises, the two teenagers now realized that the end was near, and they began to pray. This seemed to anger Robert, who shouted at them, "Quit crying, and die like men!" He then shot Mayerski in the back. At the sound of the blast, Baker's survival instinct kicked in, and rather than just kneel and wait for his turn to be killed, he got up and ran.

Robert was right on his heels, however, and shot him multiple times until he collapsed in a bloody heap. He then returned to find Mayerski still breathing, so he gave him one final shot to the head, finishing him off. After this senseless crime, Robert got in the stolen truck and drove back to his place with his brother again following behind.

Here they took a break from their mayhem and actually ate the fast food that the murdered boys had ordered but never got the chance to finish. After taking this impromptu lunch break, Robert and his brother headed to the Mira Mesa bank and robbed the place of about $2000.

Investigation and Sentence

In this case, the investigation began right after the bank robbery, when a concerned citizen followed the getaway car and told the police where the thieves were hiding. This resulted in Robert and his brother being arrested that very day. Coincidentally, one arresting officer was Michael Baker's father, Steven. Mercifully for Steven Baker, he did not even know his son had been killed at this point, so this arrest was not as traumatic for him as it otherwise would have been.

Update

In March of 1979, Robert Alton Harris was tried on two counts of murder and found guilty as charged. He was ultimately given the death sentence for his crimes. This sentence was carried out on April 21, 1992. He was reportedly given a last meal of Kentucky Fried Chicken and Domino's pizza before being marched off to the gas chamber. His last words were, "You can be a king or a street sweeper, but everybody dances with the grim reaper."

George James Trepal

Who: George James Trepal

When: October 1988

Where: Florida

Number of victims: 1

Apprehension: April 1990

Background

George Trepal is known as a classic "genius" type personality. He excelled in chemistry in college and was also a talented computer programmer. In fact, he and his wife Diana were Mensa club members, having high IQs that only approximately 2% of the human population can lay claim to. But despite all this daunting intellect, they still faced the common problems that could happen to anyone – including having to deal with bad neighbors.

Having a dispute with a neighbor is never a pleasant thing, but it happens. These situations are usually resolved amicably, and in the worst-case scenario, small claims courts can adjudicate common complaints. But when George Trepal had trouble with his neighbors, he took matters into his own hands.

He lived next to Pye and Peggy Carr, whose household boasted four children and one grandchild. They were a noisy bunch for sure, with their dog that constantly barked and kids blaring music at all times of the day. They set off fireworks for just about any occasion (fireworks on Thanksgiving? Sure! Why not?) and were frequently a nuisance. George and Diana probably had good reason to complain, but instead of going through official channels to voice his grievances, George Trepal decided to exact vengeance upon his rowdy neighbors in a horrific fashion.

The funny thing is that as much as his neighbors irked him, George never let on that they did. He was actually known to be the friendly one who would smile and wave at the Carr family, while he let his wife Diana be the attack dog sent to yell at the Carrs when they became too rambunctious. It was perhaps a classic good cop/bad cop routine, but little did they know, it would be nice guy George Trepal who would end up lethally lashing out at them.

While he continued to smile and wave, George was actually seething with animosity. His first salvo against his neighbors came in the form of an anonymous note he mailed to them. The note read "You and all your so-called family have two weeks to move out of Florida forever or else you all die. This is no joke."

Yet, apparently, that was exactly how the threatening message was perceived. Pye Carr would later recall that he shrugged it off as some kind of sick prank, and really didn't give it much more thought. The word "sick" is a bit ironic here because it was just a short time later that his wife would fall deathly ill and his entire family would be sickened to the point of death.

The Crimes

George was sick of his neighbors' trespasses and decided to use his evil genius as a chemist to solve the problem. He took Coca-Cola bottles, carefully opened them, added thallium to the mix, and then resealed them. Thallium is a tasteless, odorless poison – as little as one gram can kill an adult. Thallium has been used as a powerful pesticide in the past before it was eventually banned due to its extreme lethality.

Anyone who drank a bottle of this thallium-laced Coca-Cola would most surely die. George repeated this process on several more bottles. Now all George had to do to perpetrate his dastardly deed, was to sneak into the Carr's home and deposit the poisoned soda for the unsuspecting family members to find. This was apparently not a problem at all, since the Carrs left their doors unlocked. George just had to wait for an opportunity to drop them off undetected, and this is apparently exactly what he did.

The matriarch of the family – Peggy Carr – was the first to exhibit symptoms. She was at her job at the Nicholas Family Restaurant when she began to have chest pains. Her daughter Cissy was also employed at the restaurant, and when Peggy began to feel ill, it was to Cissy that she turned. She told her daughter that she feared she just might be having a heart attack. But instead of immediately going to the hospital, Peggy went home. Once home, the pain only became worse, and soon enough her husband had to take her to the hospital.

As she writhed in agony on a stretcher in the ER, she told the attending physician that she felt like she was on fire. But since thallium poisoning is so hard to identify, those who examined Peggy initially were quite puzzled as to what was actually transpiring. One even seemed to suggest that her issues were psychological rather than physical, referring to them as being psychosomatic. It must have been excruciating for Peggy to not only be in very real and intense pain, but to also have the so-called experts dismiss her turmoil as being nothing more than her imagination.

After this first visit, she was sent home without much advice other than to get some rest. After only a few days she would be back, complaining of even more intense symptoms. It was only then that a quick-thinking physician – Dr. Robert Vanhook – came to the conclusion that Peggy had been poisoned. This doctor even correctly guessed what poison it most likely was; he openly speculated to his colleagues that he thought it was thallium.

And he knew how to prove it. He requested and received a urine sample from Peggy, and had it tested in a lab. And sure enough, the results came back positive for thallium.

It's great that an open-minded physician finally figured out what was wrong with Peggy, but it was already too late for her. She would soon slip into a coma and die.

Her other family members, while not quite as ill, also began exhibiting symptoms of poisoning and would have to receive emergency treatment in order to avoid the same fate. It was then that the matter was brought to the attention of authorities and an investigation began.

Investigation and Sentence

After it became clear that the Carr family had been poisoned, the first step of the investigation entailed finding the source of the poising. Police searched the Carrs' home and sent several items out for lab analysis. Among these were a few empty Coca-Cola bottles (from an 8-pack found in the Carrs' kitchen) that were found to contain thallium.

Now that they knew the source of the poisoning, they had to figure out who put the poisonous cola in the home in the first place. It wasn't long before they zeroed in on George and Diana. Diana was the initial suspect, since she had been the one who was the most vocal about her dislike of the Carrs. But upon questioning George Carr, police soon began to suspect that perhaps he was the one behind the whole thing.

George was extremely nervous when police questioned him and seemed unable to look detectives in the eye. This, of course, does not necessarily mean someone is a killer, some folks are just nervous – and especially so when confronted by police – but detectives just had a hunch that there was more to George than he was letting on. They were especially suspicious when they asked George why someone might poison their neighbors. At this point, George gave one of his only confident answers, in which he unabashedly remarked that maybe it was because somebody wanted the Carrs to leave the neighborhood.

Suspicions aroused, police began to monitor George and Diana. But the real breakthrough came months later, when George and Diana moved into a new house and began renting out their old one.

Detective Susan Goreck, posing as a prospective tenant, entered into an agreement with Diana to rent their old home. This, of course, was just a front to gain access to the property. Once there, it was discovered that George had left a wide variety of suspicious chemical compounds behind in the garage. The real smoking gun came, however, when a bottle with a white powdery residue was discovered. The residue was tested and identified as thallium. This finding, along with offhand incriminating statements George had made, provided enough circumstantial evidence to lead to George's arrest.

Police stormed George and Diana Trepal's new home on April 7, 1990. As usual, Diana tried to be the assertive one in the relationship. She came to the door as police demanded entry. She tried to stop the officers from coming inside, but they were able to push her out of the way. Once inside, they then found George standing at the top of a staircase in nothing more than a pair of bikini brief underwear, asking them if he could at least get dressed.

Upon being taken into custody, George seemed to know that the jig was up. And it was. He was arraigned on charges of murder and made to stand trial in January of 1991. The trial came to a close that March, and on March 6, 1991, George Trepal was found guilty as charged and sentenced to death.

Update

In more recent years, some doubt has been cast upon this case. Peggy's daughter Cissy has theorized that perhaps it wasn't George Trepal who killed her mother, but rather Pye Carr. Nevertheless, as of this writing, George Trepal remains on death row for the murder of Peggy Carr.

Karla Faye Tucker

Who: Karla Faye Tucker
When: 1983
Where: Texas
Number of victims: 2
Apprehension: 1983

Background

Karla Tucker was born in Houston, Texas, the youngest of three girls. Her parents' marriage was not a happy one, and Karla started hanging out with the wrong crowd at a young age. It's said that she was having sex by the time she was in middle school and had left school completely by the age of 14. Leaving the normal life of an adolescent girl behind, she turned to the streets and began doing drugs and turning tricks. In this seedy underworld, she met a guy named Daniel Garrett. Garrett was a biker, and several years older than Tucker. With Garrett, Tucker truly began her life of crime.

The Crimes

On June 13, 1983, Garrett and Tucker conducted a home invasion against a fellow biker, Jerry Lynn Dean, to rob the man of his prized possession: a motorcycle he had been busy rebuilding. They gained access to Jerry Dean's apartment around three in the morning, using a key that Tucker says she found.

Fueled by drugs and alcohol, the heist was a bit odd. Tucker apparently stormed into the man's bedroom and jumped on top of the startled resident. She allegedly sat on him, and when the startled man tried to push her off, Garrett came in and hit Jerry Dean in the head with a ball-peen hammer.

With Dean knocked out by the hammer blows, Garrett grabbed some expensive motorcycle parts and loaded them in his vehicle. Tucker, meanwhile, remained with Dean, who was now clinging to life. She reportedly heard him making a gurgling sound, and to stop this bothersome noise, she grabbed a pickaxe and started striking him with it.

Garrett came back into the room, picked up the ax, and struck the struggling man one final time. He was now dead. Garrett then loaded some more stolen goods into his vehicle.

At this point, Tucker realized that someone else was present. Hiding under a pile of covers was a friend of Dean's – Deborah Ruth Thornton. Tucker, wanting to satisfy her bloodlust, began to attack Ms. Thornton. She managed to hit her a few times in the shoulder with the pickaxe before Garrett came charging in and broke the two up. It's not clear if Garrett intended to show mercy and spare the woman, but when Karla raised the ax and attacked her for a second time, he didn't intervene.
Tucker then proceeded to hit Deborah several more times, eventually tearing a hole in the woman's heart. Tucker would later claim that she had intense orgasms with each blow she struck. It's unclear if such salacious details from the mouth

of this deranged killer are true – but they were certainly duly noted during her trial.

Investigation and Sentence

The investigation into the crimes of Karla Tucker began the day after they had occurred when one of Jerry Dean's friends walked into his buddy's home and saw the horribly disfigured corpses left to rot on the floor. Because Tucker and Garrett didn't even try to cover their tracks, it didn't take long for police to be on their trail. They were arrested and charged with murder. In September of 1983, Garrett and Tucker were both charged with murder and put on trial for their crimes.

Initially, Tucker was charged with the murders of both Dean and Thornton, but she had not actually killed Dean. Though she had attacked and injured him, it was Garrett who had hit the man in the head with the ax, ending his life. Technically speaking, Karla had only murdered Deborah. She was given the chance to have one murder charge dropped if she agreed to testify about how Garrett had killed Dean.

While Karla Tucker was on trial for Deborah Thornton's murder, she allegedly had a religious experience. According to Tucker, she had been given a Bible through a special prison ministry program. Alone in her cell, she opened the Good Book and began to read. She would later claim that she didn't know what she was reading, but she soon found herself praying for God's forgiveness.

Although the more cynical among us might feel skeptical about sudden prison conversions, Karla maintained that her new faith in God was real. She became a serious Christian and even eventually married the prison minister, Reverend Dana Lane Brown. Some might wonder if this was all a stunt to show that she was a changed person in the hope of leniency, but if this was the case, it was to no avail. Due to the egregious and particularly cruel way Tucker had killed Thornton, the jury demanded nothing short of a sentence of death.

Tucker did indeed try to play up her prison conversion, hoping for a last-minute reversal of this decision. She stated that she was on drugs when she committed the crimes, and they had contributed to her bad decisions. She also tried to get support from Christian leaders by maintaining that she had turned her life around and was a changed person.

At one point, even famed Christian Broadcast Network founder Pat Robertson tried to intervene on her behalf. But other hardliners in Texas refused to budge. And in 1998, when it was time to finally carry out Karla's sentence, the then-governor of Texas, George W. Bush, ordered that the execution proceed as scheduled.

Karla Faye Tucker was executed on February 3, 1998, by lethal injection. She made history in Texas: she was the first female inmate to have her death sentence carried out in 135 years.

Update

In 2007, President George W. Bush was considering a pardon for former White House staffer, Scooter Libby, whom he viewed as having been handed a harsh sentence. For some, this provoked memories of Karla Faye Tucker, for it was under Bush's watch when he was governor of Texas that she was executed – despite repeated appeals by many prominent members of the public for mercy. Bush steadfastly refused.

Joseph Carl Shaw

Who: Joseph Carl Shaw

When: 1977

Where: South Carolina

Number of victims: 3

Apprehension: 1977

Background

Joseph Carl Shaw was born in 1955 and grew up in Louisville, Kentucky. He seemed an ordinary boy; he went to a Catholic school, did his homework, and played on the football team. He also went to church regularly, where he served as an altar boy.

However, he didn't graduate from high school. Instead, he joined the army and trained to join the military police. Graduating in 1975, he was assigned a post at South Carolina's Fort Jackson. With his army buddies there, Joseph would begin drinking and experimenting with drugs.

Joseph met and began dating a lady he's said to have been was completely infatuated with. To Joseph's chagrin, however, his girlfriend walked out on him in the fall of 1977. This triggered a series of events that would send this maniac on a deadly downward spiral.

The Crimes

Fresh from being dumped, Joseph Carl Shaw found himself in the mood for revenge. Not revenge against the woman who dumped him, but a malicious intention to cause harm to an unsuspecting society in general.

Joseph and his buddies, James Roach, Ronald Mahaffey, and Robert Williams, were allegedly driving around looking for a woman to rape when they came across Betty Swank. Hiding their devious intentions, they politely offered to give her a ride.

As soon as Betty made the unfortunate decision to get in the car, she had a gun pointed in her face. Betty, the mother of an 18-month-old son, was then taken to a remote location where she was sexually assaulted and then killed by Joseph Shaw. When he was through with his victim, he callously tossed her corpse onto the grounds of a mobile home park.

Shortly after this brutal crime, three of the previous offenders – Shaw, Roach, and Mahaffey – began plotting another. They drove around once again looking for a woman to rape, and this time they came upon Carlotta Hartness (age 14) and her boyfriend, Thomas Taylor (age 17), at a baseball diamond. The couple was simply sitting in the car talking when Joseph pulled his vehicle up next to theirs.

Roach pulled a gun on Thomas Taylor and told him to hand over all his cash. Taylor did as he was directed, but sadly, money was not all these creeps were after. While Roach had his gun trained on Thomas, the others grabbed his girlfriend and shoved her into the back of Joseph's car. Joseph then told Roach to shoot Taylor. He complied. As the terrified woman screamed in anguish to see her boyfriend shot dead, slumped behind the wheel, the murderers peeled out of the parking lot to commit even more dastardly deeds.

They took Carlotta Hartness to a desolate spot where they gang-raped her before both Roach and Shaw shot her. It is said that it was Shaw who actually killed Hartness when he shot her in the head. After this, they hopped in the car, left Hartness where she lay and went back to where they had shot Thomas – apparently to make sure that he was really dead.

Later that night, Shaw then went back to Carlotta Hartness' body so he could abuse her some more, even after she was dead. And when Carlotta's remains were eventually discovered, her brutalized corpse bore this fact out.

Investigation and Sentence

Considering that such a bloody trail of evidence was left behind, it didn't take long for police to track down the perpetrators. By November 3rd, 1977, they were all thrown behind bars. All three of them would ultimately face counts of murder, kidnapping, rape, and armed robbery.

Shaw's and Roach's actions were considered the most egregious, and it was determined that they merited death. Ronald Mahaffey managed to avoid the death penalty by taking the stand and testifying for the prosecution of Shaw and Roach. Considering the evidence against them, the two murderers were finally convinced to plead guilty.

Perhaps they thought they could avoid the death penalty by doing so, but this was not the case. Instead, on December 16, 1977, they were both given a death sentence. Shaw died in the electric chair on January 11th, 1985, when he was 29 years old. His accomplice Roach was executed a year later.

For his part in the rape and murder of Betty Swank, Robert Williams received a life sentence.

Update

This case has no updates at this time.

Timothy Joseph McGhee

Who: Timothy Joseph McGhee

Nickname: Eskimo

When: Late 1990s to Early 2000s

Where: California

Number of victims: 12 (at least)

Apprehension: 2003

Background

Timothy came into this world on April 27, 1973, the son of Scottish and Mexican immigrants. His father left when he was just a little kid, moving all the way to Alaska and never looking back. This was a terrible blow to the boy, who would always be affected by his father's absence.

Eventually, gang life would fill the void his father left. McGhee was recruited to join the Toonerville Rifa 13 gang. With this outfit, he would go on to kill an estimated 12 people between 1997 and 2001.

His first major stint behind bars took place in 1994 when he assaulted a policeman. For this crime, he was sentenced to serve four years in prison – but he was out on parole after three. While out on parole, McGhee shot several people, allegedly killing three.

The Crimes

McGhee's first known murder was Ronnie Martin, a rival gang member, though it would take several years for McGhee to be linked to this crime. Meanwhile, he was back in prison before the end of 1997, and he wouldn't get out until the spring of 1999.

Upon his release, he stayed with his grandmother, who lived in the San Gabriel Valley. McGhee is said to have shot a couple of rap artists and their bodyguard in October of 1999 outside the gates of a music studio called "Echo Sounds." McGhee apparently burst onto the scene and opened fire on the bodyguard – Dwayne "Draws" Dupree –first, before firing at hip hop mogul Ricardo "Kurupt" Brown. Draws Dupree was killed in the melee and several others were injured.

McGhee's next victim was a rival gang member, Ryan Gonzalez, whom he shot dead on June 3, 2000, after spotting the guy walking home from a party. McGhee would be linked to this crime, but it would be a few years before he would be brought into custody.

In the meantime, McGhee broadened his trespasses, and in the summer of 2000, he ambushed Carlos Langarica and Thomas Baker – Los Angeles police officers. The cops were on duty, driving around in the early morning hours, looking for a robbery suspect. They spotted the suspect's car and were attempting to follow him when they were led into the heart of McGhee's gang turf. McGhee heard about their presence on a police scanner and set up the ambush.

He directed his gang members to place a bicycle in the middle of the street, forcing the police car to swerve. This brought the officers in view of two gunmen, who began shooting. Nevertheless, these brave officers continued following the suspect's vehicle and rammed the back of their car to bring them to a halt. Once pulled over, the passenger bailed out and ran off – but another passenger in the back of the car pulled out a submachine gun and began to shoot at the police. The cops had no choice but to run for cover.

Hiding behind a tree, they continued to fire at their attackers. Thankfully for these officers, reinforcements arrived on the scene, and together, they managed to subdue and take these thugs into custody. McGhee would eventually be charged with attempted murder due to the role he played in setting up this ambush.

Another of McGhee's crimes is believed to have occurred on the 14th of September, 2000, when high schooler Marty Gregory was gunned down. It remains unclear why he was shot; the teenager was simply minding his own business, drawing a sketch of the Los Angeles River when he was killed. Also murdered was a panhandler who was nearby, David Lamont Martin, who may have been killed simply because he saw what happened.

After this spate of killings, McGhee's next murder victim was a 21-year-old man named Manuel Apodaca. Mr. Apodaca was a member of a rival gang, which is apparently why McGhee shot up his vehicle as he was driving with his pregnant girlfriend next to him. Apodaca was killed, but his girlfriend and child would survive.

This murder was followed by another when, in July of 2001, Carlos Velaso, a 21-year-old warehouse worker, was shot by McGhee's henchmen, apparently on his orders.

The next to suffer at McGhee's murderous hands was Cheri Wisotsky. Wisotsky had called the police on McGhee for dealing drugs and was then killed by McGhee in reprisal. McGhee also killed Wisotsky's mother, Mary Ann Wisotsky, as well as a neighbor named Bryham Robinson, simply for being witnesses to his crime.

After this, he then ambushed another gang member named Duane Natividad. Mr. Natividad was in the car with his girlfriend, Marjorie Mendoza, and his friend Erica Rhee. Mendoza was killed in the gunfire.

The next victim in this murder spree would be a friend of Mendonza's – Christina Duran. McGhee had learned that she was trying to report him to the police for the crime, and so he wanted her dead. He shot her in the head multiple times.

Investigation and Sentence

By 2003, Timothy McGhee was under heavy observation by investigators, and in early February he was brought into police custody. While he was awaiting trial, McGhee marshaled respect among his fellow inmates, and soon was a top gang leader behind bars. Using his clout, he managed to spark a riot. Several officers were injured, and one was almost killed. Timothy McGhee finally stood trial in 2007, and in October of that year, he was found guilty as charged. A couple of years later, in 2009, he was sentenced to death.

Update

On March 13, 2019, a moratorium on death sentences was instituted by Governor Gavin Newsom, in which all death row prisoners were granted a reprieve. Timothy McGhee remains in prison. Demonstrating how dangerous this man is, his stay has been periodically punctuated by sudden acts of violence against both fellow inmates and staff.

Emilia Carr

Who: Emilia Carr
Nickname:
When: 2009
Where: Florida
Number of victims: 1
Apprehension: 2009

Background

Emilia Carr was born on August 4, 1984, the second of three sisters. As a teenager, she told authorities that she had been abused by her father, but she later retracted her statement. When she was twenty years old, her father was charged and convicted of trying to hire someone to murder Emilia, her mother, and one of her sisters. He was given four years in prison.

By the time she was 24, Carr had been married twice and had three children. In 2008, she became engaged to Joshua Fulgham, and entangled in a love triangle that would end with a brutal murder.

Josh Fulgham and Heather Strong had been seeing each other since they were teenagers, and they had two kids together. As the relationship progressed, however, it had become common for the pair to break up, stay apart for a while, and then get back together. During one of these breaks, in the summer of 2008, Strong moved in with a mutual friend of hers and Josh Fulgham's – Benjamin McCollum.

McCollum had two kids of his own and he had made an arrangement with Strong that she would earn her keep by serving as a kind of live-in babysitter. One can only imagine Josh Fulgham's reaction when he learned that his ex was living with his old buddy Benjamin. Josh no doubt suspected that Heather was probably closer to Benjamin than they let on, and sure enough, a few weeks after Heather moved in, the pair became boyfriend and girlfriend.

Nevertheless, Josh seemed to move on, and he started to see other women himself. One of those other women was Emilia Carr. As mentioned, Ms. Carr seemed to be deeply in love with Josh, and was soon pregnant. Emilia, who already had three kids, found herself clinging to Josh Fulgham all the more. They were soon engaged to be married.

So when Josh began to drift back toward his old flame, Heather Strong, Emilia became understandably concerned. In December of 2008, her fears were realized when Josh suddenly informed her that she had to pack her things and move out. Josh had apparently decided to welcome Heather back into his life. Emilia was absolutely devastated by this turn of events.

By the end of the month, Josh had gone so far as to marry Heather Strong. But despite Emilia's fears, this relationship was not meant to last. Just a week into the marriage, Strong called the cops on Josh during a domestic disturbance in which Josh pointed a gun at her. This got Josh busted for "assault with a deadly weapon" and put him behind bars.

During his incarceration, Emilia Carr went to see him, and then she began to visit him faithfully as he served his time. Carr also tried to engineer a means to get her man out of jail by approaching Heather herself and asking her to write a letter on Fulgham's behalf.

Strong was not receptive to the idea, however, and Carr became increasingly frustrated with her. At one point she confronted Heather about signing the letter and became physical with her. Carr allegedly grabbed Heather by the hair and put a knife to her throat, demanding that she write a letter asking for Josh to be released. Emilia was heavily pregnant at the time, so it must have looked pretty strange to see this pregnant mother threatening another woman like this.

Fortunately, another mutual friend of this cast of characters, James Acome, saw what was happening and intervened. Mr. Acome had actually dated Emilia himself in the past and it was believed that he was the father of one of her other kids. In January of 2009, Emilia would turn to Acome with a plan to kill Heather in exchange for $500 from the tax return that she expected to receive that year.

Yes, Emilia was so desperate to be rid of her rival that she was actually going to try and hire a hitman with her tax return money. Fortunately, she was unable to find anyone willing to go through with the deed.
Rather than kill Strong, by the end of the month, Acome actually began to date her, and the couple was living together by January 26th.

It's amazing how fast things moved among these people, considering that it was exactly a month prior, on December 26th, that Heather Strong had married Josh Fulgham. And as this rapidly developing soap opera continued to unfold, just a week after Strong hooked up with Acome, Josh Fulgham finally received his get-out-of-jail-free card and was released into his mother's custody.

It's said that on February 15th, Josh got his mother to help him compose a letter which indicated that Heather Strong was giving him full custodial rights to their kids. He intended to get Heather to sign this document. Most who knew Heather would never think she would sign away her rights to her children, but Josh was determined to force the issue.

Acome, meanwhile, returned home to find Heather Strong missing. Shortly afterward, he got a call from Josh Fulgham himself, who bluntly informed him that Heather had come back to him.

This just didn't add up. Why would Heather leave without telling anyone? As the suspicion began to grow, Heather's cousin Misty called the police to file a missing person report.

The Crimes

It would later be revealed that Fulgham and Carr had concocted a scheme to murder Strong. Fulgham's motive was to get revenge for his arrest, as well as to get custody of his kids. For Carr, the motive was simply to get Heather out of the picture completely – eliminate her romantic rival once and for all.

The same day Josh wrote the letter for his ex-wife Heather to sign, stating that she would give up her custodial rights, he and Emilia Carr went into action. Fulgham apparently tricked Heather Strong into showing up at an old trailer with the promise of being able to steal from Emilia. It seems that Heather agreed to meet up with Josh at this remote locale to get the money. Little did she know that Emilia herself was there, ready to confront her.

When Josh and Heather stepped into the trailer, Emilia emerged behind them. Heather was immediately alarmed to see Emilia and tried to get away. Emilia blocked her exit, however, and Josh grabbed her and prevented her escape. Josh then tried to tie Heather to a chair, but Heather – by now hysterical with fear and adrenaline – broke out of her bonds and tried desperately once again to get out.

But Josh got control of her again, and this time, Emilia took the initiative. She taped Heather to the chair, wrapping duct tape around her torso several times until she couldn't free herself. Heather was terrified and began to plead with her captors to let her go. At this point, Josh put the child custody letter in front of Heather's face and demanded that she sign it.

After she signed the paper, things got even worse for Heather. Josh took out a heavy metal flashlight and hit Heather in the head with it. He then put a garbage bag on her head and Emilia put duct tape around Heather's neck to tighten the bag so that Heather's air supply would be cut off.

When she didn't suffocate fast enough for Emilia's liking, however, Emilia took the initiative and tried to break Heather's neck. This effort was not successful.

Finally, Josh covered Strong's mouth and nose with his hands until she died. The murderous duo then left the trailer to go about their business as though nothing happened. It was a full two days later before Josh returned to the site to bury Heather's corpse, and a month before she would be found in a shallow grave nearby.

Investigation and Sentence

It didn't take long for investigators to zero in on Josh Fulgham as a suspect. It was Josh, after all, who had called up Heather's boyfriend the very day of her disappearance to tell him that Heather was back with him. Detectives questioned Josh and he ended up confessing what had been done, but he insisted that Emilia was the real killer, and he had only helped her.

Meanwhile, upon being questioned, Emilia put all the blame on Josh. She loved the man dearly, but she was more than ready to flip on him when it came to her being charged with murder. The evidence spoke for itself, and the subsequent autopsy told a gruesome tale. It corroborated much of the accusations that the two lovers aimed at each other, and it seemed to confirm that they were both responsible for Heather's death.

As such, both Emilia and Josh were arrested on charges of kidnapping and murder. The real evidence against Emilia, however, would be gleaned while she was awaiting trial. The police had managed to break into Emilia's inner circle when Josh Fulgham's sister, Michele Gustafson, decided to talk to the police. Fulgham's sister had apparently become a confidante for Emilia, and she would often speak quite freely with her.

Unbeknownst to Emilia, the police got Josh's sister to agree to record her conversations with Emilia, while still portraying herself as that same loyal friend Emilia could turn to. Soon enough, Emilia began talking, and the recorded conversations were quite revelatory. Initially, she claimed ignorance about the whole thing, but her version of events rapidly changed the more she talked.

Soon she was telling Fulgham's sister that she knew what Josh had done and that he had murdered Heather. This inside knowledge then morphed into Emilia claiming that she had stumbled upon Heather's dead body. In another call, she altered her remembrance of events further by saying she not only saw the dead body but that she was there to witness Josh killing Heather.

Then, slowly but surely, she began to open up and confess that she too, had helped to kill Heather. Her final descriptions of the crime were so accurate that they could be used in court to verify the evidence that investigators had uncovered at the scene.
Emilia Carr's trial commenced on December 1, 2010. The recorded telephone admission, coupled with the testimony of former friends whom Emilia had directly tried to hire to carry out a hit on Heather, and the contributions of those who

witnessed the episode in which Emilia pulled a knife on the deceased, resulted in a damning body of evidence.

It didn't take long for the jury to render a guilty verdict, and it wasn't much of a surprise when they recommended that she be sentenced to death. On February 22, 2011, Judge Willard Pope delivered the official sentence: life imprisonment for kidnapping, and the death sentence for murder. The only sentence that mattered, of course, was the death sentence, which placed her on death row.

Interestingly, Joshua Fulghum was not sentenced to death. He was given a life sentence with no possibility of parole.

Update

Emilia's stint on death row came to an end on May 19, 2017, when she was re-sentenced to life without parole.

Darlie Routier

Who: Darlie Routier

When: June 6, 1996

Where: Texas

Number of victims: 2

Apprehension: 1996

Background

Darlie Routier grew up in the conservative confines of Texas. She was a married woman with three little boys – Damon, Devon, and baby Drake. She and her husband Darin were high school sweethearts and got married at a young age. They both worked hard and tried their best to get by. Life was good for the family until the night Damon, Devon, and Darlie all sustained stab wounds.

The Crimes

On the night of June 6, 1996, Darlie Routier called 911 to report that her family had been attacked by a knife-wielding maniac. According to her, a man had broken into her home and assaulted her and two of her sons before running out of the house.

Random acts of violence are unusual – but they do happen. Sometimes it's a robbery gone wrong, and other times, the killer may be mentally ill or on drugs. And sometimes there is just no reason we can fathom.

And this is precisely what Darlie was suggesting occurred when she called 911 to report that someone had broken into her home, stabbed her and her two little boys, and then ran off. To her, what had happened was clear, but once the investigation began, not everyone would be convinced that she was the victim – but rather, the killer herself.

Investigation and Sentence

The cops arrived at Darlie's house just moments after she called for help. Upon their arrival, they found that a window screen in her garage was sliced open as if this were how the attacker had made their way into Darlie's home. The police then searched the immediate area surrounding the house hoping to flush out the assailant, but there was no sign of anyone in the immediate vicinity.

Police questioned Darlie at the scene. She claimed that she had dozed off on the living room sofa with little Damon and Devon next to her. She was then woken up a few hours later by the commotion of someone in her house. Darlie claimed she had confronted the man, and he got up and ran out of the house, dropping the knife in a utility room before he made his exit.

The police immediately found Darlie's story suspicious. For one thing, Darlie claimed that the intruder had both broken in and then left her home through the garage. To the police, the slit screen looked staged, and besides this bogus bit of staging, there was no indication that anyone had actually climbed through the window after the screen had been cut. There was a flower bed right under that garage window, and you would think that if someone was climbing up into a window and then jumping out of the window, they would have stepped all over the flowers, and kicked up a bunch of dirt and debris. However, the garden below the window hadn't been disturbed.

The more they looked into matters, the more and more likely it seemed that there was no intruder in the first place – that Darlie had killed her own kids, injured herself, and then very amateurishly tried to stage a home invasion that never actually occurred.

After Darlie was released from the hospital, some of her behavior was also deemed suspicious by investigators. The most infamous incident was no doubt the "silly string" moment at the gravesite of her slain sons. On June 14th, 1996, her freshly buried son Devon would have turned seven years old, just seven days after the murder.

To commemorate the date, Darlie went to the grave to celebrate. This incident was captured on camera, and the video shows Darlie happily celebrating, spraying silly string onto her slain sons' graves. She would later explain that she just wanted to make the best of a terrible situation, knowing that her son would have wanted to celebrate his birthday. But once this incident was picked up by the media, they were highly judgmental and began to show Darlie as a callous and uncaring mother, happily dancing on her children's graves.

Then – as now – the media had a powerful role in manipulating the public's perception.

And although Darlie herself was injured in the alleged attack, investigators were highly suspicious of how she had received those injuries. She had wounds to her arm and neck that would later be determined to be self-inflicted. They were even referred to as being superficial, yet some reports stated that one of the wounds on her arm had cut her to the bone.

Nevertheless, it would be speculated that the whole thing was staged, and Darlie had killed her own kids, perhaps as a response to financial difficulties. Darlie had in fact, taken out life insurance policies on her children. Although it's said that the amount she would receive for them would barely have been able to cover the cost of funeral arrangements, let alone pay off her debts.

Nevertheless, Darlie was arrested on June 18th, 1996, and stood trial for capital murder shortly thereafter. The following year, in February of 1997, she was convicted, and sentenced to death. As of this writing (in the early 2020s) Darlie still sits on death row, awaiting her fate.

Update

Ever since her arrest, conviction, and death sentence, Darlie has maintained that she is innocent. She has steadfastly insisted that she would never have intentionally hurt her sons. She sticks to her story that someone broke in and stabbed her and her little boys. She has appealed her sentence several times over the years, but her appeals have always been rejected. Meanwhile, if the killer was just someone who burst into her home that summer night, they have never been caught.

Spencer Goodman

Who: Spencer Goodman
Nickname:
When: July 2, 1991
Where: Texas and Colorado
Number of victims: 1
Apprehension: 1991

Background

By the time he was in his early 20s, Spencer was a career criminal. He had been arrested for robbery and a whole litany of other crimes, yet due to the "revolving prison doors" of Texas, at the time, his sentences were usually brief and it wasn't long before he was out on parole. One day after his parole release in the summer of 1991, Spencer would cross paths with Cecile Ham.

Ms. Ham was 48 years old at the time and was the wife of prominent Texan Bill Ham, who worked as the manager for the rock band ZZ Top. Cecile was simply out doing some shopping on July 2nd when she was intercepted by Spencer. Spencer had noticed her flashy red Cadillac, and – according to his later testimony – he was simply tired of walking so he decided to commandeer the vehicle.

The Crime

Cecile Ham had stopped at a local pharmacy to call home at around 4:30 in the afternoon. Her maid picked up the phone, and Cecile said she would be back from her shopping trip soon, telling her she just had to make a stop at the bank before she headed home. This quick call was the last time anyone would hear from Cecile Ham.

Shortly after she placed this call, Cecile Ham was confronted by Goodman, who had been watching her the whole time. He had seen her pull up in the flashy car and use the payphone in front of the pharmacy. As soon as she got into the car, Goodman made his move.

He walked right up to her driver's side door, opened it, and punched her in the face with tremendous force. This punch apparently knocked her out, and after that, Goodman simply pushed her over into the passenger seat while he got behind the wheel and took off. Goodman claimed that he drove to a remote spot, where he broke the woman's neck. Goodman insisted that she was still unconscious at the time as if to clarify that she didn't feel any pain.

Once she was dead, Goodman claims that he put her corpse in the trunk, shut it, and spent the next several hours aimlessly driving around before finding somewhere to dump her body.

After several hours passed without any sign of Cecile, her worried husband notified the police that his wife might be missing. The police then sent out a missing person bulletin, complete with a description of both Cecile and her prized red Cadillac. The investigation began.

Investigation and Sentence

Initially, investigators theorized that Cecile may have been kidnapped by someone who knew who her husband was, and who was planning to hold her for ransom. However, this idea was quickly discarded when it became clear that Mr. Ham was not receiving any demands from the kidnapper.

As time passed, this began to look more and more like a random crime. The first real lead that investigators received were some credit card transactions that Spencer made after killing Cecile and taking her car.

Just a couple of hours after hits were registered as coming from Cecile's card, a witness described a man who was using that very credit card at a local Houston area gas station. The guy was described as being a tall, muscular young man who was pumping gas into a red Cadillac. According to the witnesses, the man was alone, which of course only deepened the concern of investigators. Because if this man was using Cecile's credit cards and driving her car – well then, where was Cecile?

Nevertheless, investigators took note of the man's physical description. He was said to be in his mid-20s and around six feet tall. At this point in the investigation, helicopters were dispatched over Houston in search of both the red Cadillac and the mystery man seen driving it. As soon as a ping came in that he had used the credit card, investigators would swoop (sometimes literally) down to try and intercept him. Yet somehow or other, the young man kept right on eluding them.

And then, on the 10th of July, the trail seemed to go cold entirely. There were no more pings on the credit card to track. Where was the suspect? A few clues came in from surveillance videos in local stores that had managed to capture the young man on camera. Once the still images from these cameras were released to the public, investigators were contacted by an individual who claimed to know the man, and furthermore, to know where he stayed.

According to the tipster, the guy was actually staying – of all places – at a Christian youth camp in Marble Falls, Texas. According to those at the camp, Spencer earned his keep doing odd jobs. He was generally described as a nice guy, but at least one female camper complained that he had harassed her. He had also stolen a credit card from someone there.

This proved to be the real key, and police quickly put out a nationwide alert on the card so they could swarm in the second he used it. That moment came on the 7th of August – not in Texas – but in Basalt, Colorado. After leaving the camp, the suspect had apparently traveled fairly far. Nevertheless, thanks to the alert, as soon as Goodman used the card, the police were notified.

Goodman was in the parking lot when a police car pulled up. Seeing the police, he quickly hopped into his vehicle and peeled out of the lot. This led to a high-speed chase which was fortunately brief. Spencer had traveled about 30 miles at about 100 miles an hour before swerving off an embankment and crashing. Goodman was lucky to have survived with only very slight injuries. He was briefly held at a hospital before he was patched up and put behind bars.

Once he was in police custody, Goodman began to openly discuss what he had done to Cecile Ham. Without hesitation, he described how he killed her, put her in the trunk of her own car, drove to a remote location, and then disposed of her body. He even led them to her remains, which were decaying, but were identified by the jewelry that she had worn. Goodman, in the meantime, was charged with capital murder and remained in jail, waiting to stand trial.

His day in court arrived in May 1992. During the trial, his lawyers tried to make the argument that while Goodman took full responsibility for his actions, he did not mean to kill Cecile Ham. According to them, the actual murder was an accident. It was a bit of a stretch to argue that someone accidentally broke another human being's neck, but this was the case made by Goodman's defense. They thought that if they could raise doubt as to Goodman's intentions, he could at least beat the death penalty. But this was not to be. The sentence delivered would indeed be death, and it would be carried out in full in 2000.

Update

Cecile's husband, Bill Ham, passed away on June 20th, 2016. His friends from ZZ Top gave the man whom they viewed as a powerful part of their band's successful formula a glowing tribute. He was remembered as a great musician and manager but above all a man who always loved and cherished the memory of his slain wife, Cecile. Their friends and family can only hope that these soul mates have finally been reunited.

The Last Resort

Just as any judge would tell you, dealing someone a death sentence is never an easy thing. For those of us with a good conscience and a strong moral compass, ending someone's life is not a choice taken lightly. A good judge tasked with such a heavy decision must weigh all the circumstances of the case, making sure that the decision is just.

It is for precisely this reason that in the United States of America—a country of some 330 million people—that the death penalty is so rare. About half of all states have either abolished it or have a moratorium on executions. Still, there are times and circumstances in which crimes committed are so terrible, the death sentence is chosen.

Death penalties are a punishment to criminals who seem unlikely to be rehabilitated, but they also serve as a reminder and a deterrent to the rest of society. One's perspective is likely to depend on how one considers the value of human life. In a utilitarian approach, authorities consider it a difficult decision that is taken when it results in the most good for the most people – when it protects the public and promotes public safety. In any case, it is the last resort.

Further Readings

Now that we've brought this book to a close, let's take a look at some of the reading and reference materials that helped make it all possible. Here you will find a wide variety of viewpoints, perspectives, and themes that were touched upon in this book. If you would like to expand your knowledge in any of these areas, feel free to browse through them for yourself.

Road Kill. David Jacobs

This book is an anthology of true crime cases involving incidents that occurred on the road. In particular, it highlights the case of Spencer Goodman who murdered Cecile Ham after seeing her pull up to a pharmacy in her red Cadillac

The Last Gasp: The Rise and Fall of the American Gas Chamber. Scott Christianson

Another anthology—this book takes a look at several death row cases. Scott Christianson provides a lot of riveting details to a wide variety of death row cases. If you would like to know more, this is a great place to start.

Buried Memories. Irene Pierce

Irene follows the life and crimes of Betty Lou Beets. This book is biographical in nature and is quite in-depth when it comes to both Betty's many marriages as well as her many murders.

Murder Inc: The Mafia's Hit Men in New York City. Graham K. Bell

True crime writer Graham K. Bell traces the history of the infamous "Murder Inc" crime syndicate. This book provides a good background on organized crime in general and eventual death row inmate, Frank Abbandando in particular.

Dateline Purgatory: Examining the Case that Sentenced Darlie Routier to Death. Kathy Cruz

As you might imagine, this book examines the case of Darlie Routier. Darlie has long denied killing her children, and in this text, author Kathy Cruz takes a more sympathetic tone. Darlie's case is an unusual one and you could quite easily argue both sides. Having that said, Kathy's book tends to lean more in favor of Darlie's plight.

Printed in Great Britain
by Amazon